# Coming From Not Knowing

FRED SPRUELL
AKA
FREDERICK RULE

BOOKSIDE Press

CW00801544

Copyright © 2025 by Fred Spruell AKA Frederick Rule

ISBN: 978-1-77883-571-1 (Paperback)

All rights reserved. No part of this publication may be reproduced, distributed, or transmitted in any form or by any means, including photocopying, recording, or other electronic or mechanical methods, without the prior written permission of the publisher, except in the case brief quotations embodied in critical reviews and other noncommercial uses permitted by copyright law.

The views expressed in this book are solely those of the author and do not necessarily reflect the views of the publisher, and the publisher hereby disclaims any responsibility for them.

BOOKSIDE Press

BookSide Press
877-741-8091
www.booksidepress.com
orders@booksidepress.com

# *Personal Story Telling*

I gave up a position as "Floor Director and Camera Operator" at KTBS Chanel 27 in Topeka Kansas, when the next step would have been a TV Director, to come to Los Angeles and pursue an acting career. After paying for acting classes, pounding the pavement, auditioning for several years, I found myself setting across the room from a Sally Powers an assistance-casting director at Screen Gems Werner Brothers studio. It became painfully clear to me that it was time to end this general interview when Sally Powers stood up and cordially asked me if I would be willing to put together a scene of about three to five minutes with another actor and come back in two weeks and perform it in front of her boss Rene Vilenta, who was head of Screen gems at Warner Brothers Studios in Burbank I sheepishly said I would be glad to and we thanked each other and I awkwardly fumbled my way out of the room.

My acting coach Jonathon Daly was very excited about writing an original scene for me and a female actor Darlene Cravioto. He came up with and idea of having me a black man have a hearing deficit in one ear and completely def in the other. Darlene the other half of the dyad a beautiful white woman has an even more extreme deficit which was blindness. The scene opens with the two of us seated beside each other on a park bench and of course neither of us are aware of the other's deficit. Darlene is also not aware that I am African heritage.

Although both Darlene and I were both very good actors the scene was very well written and tailored to our talent not to mention the richness of having a black man and white woman, each with very pronounced deficits and neither of them the least bit aware. I can only imagine what a wonderful picture they must have painted while creating strategies to deal with the wholes each of them left for the other to fill. For example, when she in advertnently turns away and he would be un able to read her lips often his response would have little or no relation to what she had said. She knows they both are engaged in a process of putting square pegs into round wholes.

Until the end they both finally figure out. He exclaims oh you're blind and she follow suit and you're deaf. Neither of them references their racial difference.

As they are walking across the parking lot in route to the casting office, they both are keenly aware that they are in possession of a very precise and very sophifiticated instrument capable of propelling either or both to stardom. I am terrified as I usually am prior to performance. Judging by the way Darlene is reacting it is obviously showing. You nervous peace of shit you better not fuck this up she yell at me. By now I am sweating bullets but I am un able to shake of the terror but I attempt to mount a retaliatory attack back at her and we carry this fight right into the office right up to the desk where we check in. They waste no time sending us in. Of course, as usual Darlene takes over and does all the talking.

Hi I am Darlene Craviotto and this is my scene partner Fred Spruell. Sally Powers greeted us hi, I am Sally Powers. She directs our attention to a in obscure corner of the room. You are going to be performing for my boss Rene Valente, who is head of Screen Gems and a couple of her assistance. There was no reaction from them, which compounded my fear. Sally Powers redirected her attention to us. This is your space you can arrange it any way you want. Take your time and start whenever you like, as she joined the other automaton like figures, with a cold, bored, persona. Their arms were all folded across their chest as if they were standing at parade rest at a military function. As we began to pace back and forth across the room. Getting no positive feed back from them and having Darlene mad at me fueled my sense of desperation, I felt terrible alone and isolated. I took a risk. I boldly stepped in front of Darlene on one of her trips pass, I stopped her and whispered it you and me against the world Darlene. When she smiled back at me that was my cue that she had accepted my offering of peace. The casting crew cold rejection s instead of further separating us had inadvertently driven us together. From start to finish we rocked.

It was as if we were doing this scene for us. It was as if we had lost our awareness of their presence in the room. When we started to hear their laughter, it was gravy I no longer felt we needed their participation for our process to be successful. When the scene ended, I was not only elated that we had done a wonderful job but I was glad it was over I no longer had to worry about possibly messing this up for Darlene. It did not take long to figure out who the big cheese in this group was, especially the way she took the lead. She walked right up to me No one else spoke. "Who is your agent"? she said to me. I do not have an agent, I responded. She could not believe her ears. "You don't have an agent"? she said. No, I said apologetically. With out hesitating she gave me a list of agents to call. Tell them I told you to call she said. Thank you I will I said. Before dropping me from her radar she looked straight into my soul and said: When something comes up that you are right for I am going to call you. Again, I said thank you. This may or may not have been the last thing she said to me but it is the last thing I remembered, "I mean it" We left the room.

Six to eight months later when I had not heard from Rene, I lumped her into the same category with the rest of the Hollywood casting directors, and would be producers. Full of promises but no delivery. It was near the end of a hot summer day in Los Angeles when the tram I was on pulled into the Tour Guide dispatch area at Universal Studios. Before we came to a stop a tour guide was running along side of the tram scream Frederick you have a message. You need to call Rene Velente, over at Warner Bros. She wants, you to come over to pick up a script so you can go over tomorrow and read for the lead in a television series.

I could not believe what I was hearing. When I walked into the dispatch area to use the phone, all the tour guides were congratulating me. Some how we all assumed it was a done deal. They all knew what a dedicated actor I was. My commitment to the trade took precedence over every thing else. After arranging to pick up the script, title "The First Family of Washington" Later to become "That's My Mama" I immediately started to fantasize about my long-awaited success. No more one room apartments, no more living of peanut butter and jelly, and above all else I could make that phone call home to my mother, telling her success has finally come and I am buying you that house you have always dreamt about.

At that moment it was as if I was awakened from a dream. It did not occur to me until that moment that there existed, a slight possibility that I might not get the part, after all this was an offer to come for an audition not the part. From that moment on my dream started to crumble. I found my self-imploding with despair instead of exploding with excitement. What if I do not get the part? all my friends will be disappointed in me. I will look like a fool. I kept trying to convince my self that I could pull my self out of this black whole. I stopped at a local restaurant in the valley, to have a cup of hot tea with honey, in order to bolster my energy. As I walked out of the restaurant and as I was waiting at the corner for the light to change in route to my appointment, a man happened to walk by head in the opposite direction. Said, excuse me sir but can it be that bad. I said, do I look bad? He said you look like you do not have a friend in the world. It was as clear to me then as it is clear to me now that I had awaken from my dream even before I had a chance to go to sleep.

# *Coming From Not Knowing*

(No fear — No hatred — No guilt — No shame)

Inside of a mask that resembles Lon Chaney

"The Phantom of The Opera"

Things seem like a mystery only because you don't understand them. As soon as you find you don't understand anything it's no longer a mystery.

The mind is like a child. You have to be very careful about what you give it to play with. I had an opportunity to operate from a space of not knowing as the Phantom in "Phantom of the Opera" at Universal Studios tour center. I was dressed in tails, a top hat, arm-length white gloves, tuxedo pants and a hideous mask that looked like Lon Chaney in the movie. It fit right over my head and rested on my shoulders, which provided me with total and complete anonymity.

Before we go on with the tour, let me tell you a little bit about why I am taking you on it.

I was born and raised in the deep-south where, as a black person, the feeling of being a non-entity, having low self-worth, seeming invisible, was perpetuated.

I am reminded of a time when I dropped out of school for a day to work in the cotton field on Senator

James O. Eastland's plantation. The required work was to chop the grass and weeds from around the cotton. However, because it began to rain we were forced to stop work and taken to the Senator's store so he could decide how much to pay us for the partial work we'd done in the field. Our normal pay was $3 for a 12-hour day but because of the rain we were paid only a fraction of that. We black women, men and children were placed in a corner on the floor of the store while white men and women came in to do their shopping. What is so disturbing to me now, as well as it was then, is that the white men and women acted as if we were invisible, i.e. they never looked in our direction or acted as if we were there. I have never felt so ashamed and humiliated in my life. I felt worthless and invisible.

In the primal stage of my advent into this space and time I began to understand the script given to me by my mother, friends, relatives, and also whites. The script said that I, Fred Spruell, was my thoughts and my body which further translated to mean that I was black, awful, ugly, smelly, dumb and had kinky hair, flat feet, blood-shot eyes, dirty, and stupid. Needless to say, I hated the script and I hated myself for accepting it.

After all my efforts to rewrite the script seemed hopeless, I absolutely wanted to die. Fearing death, as my faithful thoughts had taught me to, I was destined to live as a hopeless cripple. In spite of all my efforts to change that kind of thinking, I continued to operate from a position of thinking that all of that nonsense was true. I never thought I was enough. My entire life I was lacking the courage to take that leap of faith and risk failing. I was already the son of a falling angel and there was no place left for me to fall. Perhaps there is hope.

I am finally beginning to see that. It wasn't until I was willing to risk coming from a place of not knowing who I am, that I can even begin to know who you are. You see, all of those things that I feared might be true about myself, stand as barriers between us getting to know each other.

The early part of 1982, I went to a benefit, ("My Dinner With Andre") at the Odyssey Theater. While attending the first of five functions that were scheduled that day, I found myself deeply engrossed in a lecture given by Yuric Bogarivcz, an actor, director and teacher, who was doing extensive work in the Polish Theater. He talked about the task or barriers that an actor has to push through each time he or she begins to work.

These barriers are the choices that the actor is faced with. He/she has to decide whether to empty out the cup of all of the blocks that get in the way of his/her willingness to come from not knowing. To put it more plainly, to lie or tell the truth. "You have to be willing to tell the absolute truth in order to make a beautiful lie" to quote the famous Russian ballet dancer Baryshnikov.

Since I have studied acting for many years, this dialogue was by no means new to me. But, for some unknown reason, I saw a direct parallel between what he was saying and how I had been at both the cause and effect of coming from not knowing by simply putting on a mask.

Since I was wearing a mask, I became free of my mind and my body. I felt free to say and do just about anything that I could think of. When I entered the arena, I left behind all knowledge of good and evil. This arena was my playpen where approximately 600 tourist waited their turn to get on a tram which would take them on a tour of the Universal Studios back lot. My job was to keep their minds off of the 2 to 3 hour wait. My only prop was a platform. On the platform was a sign that read "Lon Chaney, Phantom Of The Opera, 1925".

I did the following: mechanical mime-like movements, statue-like stand with hypnotic stares, roars and monster-like guttural sounds. I also held babies and took pictures with little children, and scared the absolute life out of men and women. And I danced like Gene Kelly and Fred Astaire.

From the moment they laid eyed on me, my mere presence evoked repulsion, fear, hatred, dislike, fascination, admiration, envy, pity, and sexuality. Their reaction to me provided me with every bit of the ammunition that I could ever hope to have in my arsenal. My prowess as a predator was incredible. I was able to discern the most subtle of their communications. If there ever was a Garden of Eden this was it.

There was always an element of not knowing, me not knowing how I was going to react to them until they gave me something to react to, and they not knowing whether I Was real or imagined, until I had them firmly in my grasp. It thrilled me, oh God, how it thrilled me, to see people riveted from seemingly zero energy to instantaneous orgasmic-like twisted faces, limbs flying, legs kicking, feet stomping, men clenching their fists and bracing themselves for a slow dance on the killing ground, women throwing their purses, dropping their shades, wetting their pants, for a brief moment abandoning their children and within seconds realizing what they had done, gathering them in.

A moment after letting out a blood curdling scream, they would laugh uncontrollably and thank me for having scared them. Once I asked a lady why she had thanked me, and she replied that she was so frightened she thought she was going to die. When she realized she wasn't going to die, she felt she needed to thank me for handing her back her life.

I can't begin to tell you how it pleased me to have the power to evoke these kinds of reactions from men, women, and children from all over the world. If you could have seen the faces of those little children in a sea of hundreds of grownups of assorted shapes, sizes and colors, in a seemingly hypnotic-like trance of excitement, waiting to see another group of people come unglued. When they realized it was just a game, as life is a game, they were willing to have some fun with it.

It has provided me with some interesting insights into myself. Depending on where the elevator stops in my level of consciousness, I might look out there and see a bunch of stupid, fat, pathetic, caged animals. However, what I saw in them had more to say about me than it could ever say about them. If you take away all the reasons why you hate someone, you are left with "I love you." If you scare the living daylights out of someone, there is no time for the mind to edit their response, so you get the truth and the truth for me is I love people.

I am fascinated by them, by their accents, their colors, their languages, their bodies and their body language. I was turned on by them emotionally, mentally and physically. I got to see how cruel they could be, how kind, how loving, how caring, and, also, how unconscious.

I provided a mirror for them to see themselves and they provided a mirror for me. Together we all provided a mirror for each of us to unabashedly look into and to hear the echo that resounds throughout the universe, that hollers out to us the message "I love you, and I know you love me." I am you and you are me. And if you weren't there, I couldn't be here.

When we come from preconceived notions, life becomes distorted. I remember while working beside my mother as a young boy I asked her pointedly, "why is it that white folks ride around in beautiful cars and live in beautiful houses, while colored people work the cotton fields and live in shacks." Her response to me was, "the Cain and Abel story."

I walked away from that conversation thinking that I deserved what I was getting.

There was a period in my life when some more interesting things occurred, some life threatening. At this juncture I think it is important that I mention that I was nearly the same age as Emmett Till and lived about

15 to 20 miles from where he was brutally murdered in a small town called Money Mississippi.

I lived on a plantation outside Minter City, a town that consisted of a couple of juke joints, a cotton gin, and a movie theater. We eventually moved off the plantation to a city about 20 miles south called Green Wood, Mississippi. There I attended school at Broad Street High School. However, before getting to school, I arose at about 4 am, and waited to be picked up by a white man from the North side of the river and driven several miles to North Greenwood where we parked at a service station. He would go into the service station while I and 2 other boys prepared papers to be delivered to homes on the north side.

We rolled the papers and secured them with rubber bands and waited for him to return. When he came back to the car, an old Ford with running boards, he was almost always drunk. On one occasion, after sitting down behind the wheel, he turned and looking directly at me, said, "l jest can't understand why anybody would want to be someplace where they are not wanted. Can you?"

I boldly replied, "Yes, I can."

He started to turn away and then angrily turned back to me and asked, "What did you say?"

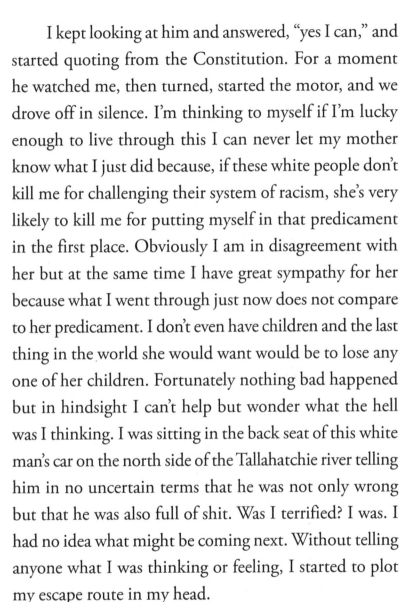

I kept looking at him and answered, "yes I can," and started quoting from the Constitution. For a moment he watched me, then turned, started the motor, and we drove off in silence. I'm thinking to myself if I'm lucky enough to live through this I can never let my mother know what I just did because, if these white people don't kill me for challenging their system of racism, she's very likely to kill me for putting myself in that predicament in the first place. Obviously I am in disagreement with her but at the same time I have great sympathy for her because what I went through just now does not compare to her predicament. I don't even have children and the last thing in the world she would want would be to lose any one of her children. Fortunately nothing bad happened but in hindsight I can't help but wonder what the hell was I thinking. I was sitting in the back seat of this white man's car on the north side of the Tallahatchie river telling him in no uncertain terms that he was not only wrong but that he was also full of shit. Was I terrified? I was. I had no idea what might be coming next. Without telling anyone what I was thinking or feeling, I started to plot my escape route in my head.

Well known psychiatrist and author, Dr. David Viscott, said in response to a caller on KABC talk radio in Los Angeles, California, that the credentials of a therapist is not nearly as important as who the person. Invariably when I say to someone that I am attending a nontraditional school does not restrict me to classroom setting, instead it gives me both the freedom and responsibility to acquire my learning on my own time and in any way I choose to get it. They always ask, "Is it accredited?" And I say, "no, but it's wonderful."

Traditional schools seem to stifle my learning and take the excitement of learning out of it. This program has allowed me to be like a child unyielding in my excitement over learning. One of the best features about this program is that there are no tests or grades to turn in. It allows a person to be an individual learning at one's own comfortable pace and not having to feel like a failure or misfit if one is a slow learner. I am a slow learner. I am deterred from expressing my fullest appreciation for this program by my limited ability to be able to express my true feeling on paper.

It is not so important what this program does for its learners, as is the opportunity it provides for its learners to do for themselves. I unequivocally chose this program over any other program that I am presently familiar with.

For me the University Without Walls program was an idea whose time has come. It came for me when I had been in therapy for about a year. One day my therapist looked me straight in the eye and said, "What is an intelligent person like you, with a great sense of humor, doing working in a Xerox room?" She suggested that I might think about becoming a therapist. She had no doubt that I would make a great therapist. After finding out that I met all the prerequisites for the UWW/Union program, she firmly suggested that I call the school and find out what I needed to do in order to get enrolled. That was the dawn of a new day in my life.

Up to that point, I was stuck in a rut. I wasn't sure about who I was, what I wanted to do, or how to go about doing it. Once I started to put together my proposed study plan for my BA degree, my life started to take shape. It was as if I was putting my life in order.

I developed a childlike compulsion for new knowledge. On evenings when we would have "cluster meetings" it was difficult to hold me down because of my eagerness to share some knowledge or new experience. There were certainly lots of interesting topics discussed that could quite easily cause someone who was genuinely eager to learn, to become overzealous. Some discussions and demonstrations that peaked my interest were neuro-linquistic programs, alcoholism, and incest.

I enrolled in a class that was supervised by Sue Oppenheimer (M.A., M.F.C.C.) on the family system.

This program gave me the impetus to get involved in everything I thought that had some value of a psychological nature. I got involved in teaching drama at the California Institute for Men and Women at Chino and, to prove that I could do anything I chose to do, I did a fire walk under the direction of Tony Robbins.

I became so self-initiated that I bought all of the psychological related books and tapes. I attended seminars. I was made aware that learning could take place in any setting. I learned from listening to the radio, watching TV, attending acting classes, and from talking and sharing experiences with total strangers on the street. My eagerness with this program has become an unending process. I have every reason in the world to believe I would become an excellent therapist.

I was co-leading a family workshop in Northern California and a young white girl about 6 or 7 years old grabbed hold of my pants, pulled on them, and said, "1 see it." I locked her hand on my leg to prevent her from putting her hand inside of my pants. I could have chosen to do a hundred and one million other things, but because I was familiar with re-evaluation cocounseling I had confidence that allowing her to act out her feelings was the right thing to do. She chose me, an African American man, to give her a session on a potential sexual abuse incident.

I remember when I was about 4 years old and I was lying on the porch, pretending to be asleep, while my mother and Aunt Teva were quilting in the house. Mother asked my Aunt "who was that man who just walked past the house?" My Aunt replied, "l don't know, but it was a colored man." A light bulb went off in my head, I must be colored since I was the same color as the man. I never understood racial distinctions, black, white, colored, before. The expression, "children are to be seen and not heard," was how black adults referred to their children. When adults talked, children were sent away to play.

www.ingramcontent.com/pod-product-compliance
Lightning Source LLC
Jackson TN
JSHW022117060225
78527JS00009B/4